This book is filled with all kinds of poems, from all kinds of inspirations, all kinds of styles and all kinds of subjects. What they have in common is Leslie's loving gaze and heart, pulling out strands of beauty. She is a beauty-miner, a beauty-weaver, and she glows because of it. Her gaze is soft and kind, her eyes sparkle, and she calls out benedictions in her home, in her writing, in her city. What a blessing God gave us when he thought up Leslie Bustard.
—KATY BOWSER HUTSON, *forming member of the band Rain for Roots and author of* Now I Lay Me Down to Fight

These poems exalt the wonders of the everyday, wonders we so often neglect. They bring inward and outward illumination to our eyes and to our hearts, encouraging us to hope, love, feel, to reach out again, and again.
—ROSS WILSON, *BEM artist/sculptor*

The poems in *The Goodness of the Lord in the Land of the Living* are beautiful and moving, written with a clear-eyed noticing and attentiveness to the smallest detail of the natural world and the people around her. Leslie invites readers into her gaze toward possibility and hopefulness. Even while acknowledging the experience of illness and the sometimes private sorrowful mysteries of life, these pieces, collectively, are a shout for joy that could ring from rooftops.
—KAREN PERIS, *singer-songwriter for* the innocence mission

Leslie Anne Bustard's poetry has a familiar feel—like moist earth on bare feet or a neighbor's warm greeting at your door when bringing over food. Her voice is clear and honest and appealing, and her imagery taken from a lived life. Nothing forced or feigned. Nothing overworked or showy. There's sadness. There's laughter. And one word seems to hang in the air from every page:

joy—unalloyed joy. Not happiness, but something sturdy and stronger and able to move through shadows and loss.

There are lots of butterflies here—it's a garden after all. But there are also clouds and bare trees. While reading through her whole cycle of the seasons, her responses to paintings and to the poetry of others, one senses that the poet knows this place and has a homing signal for it. It's the meeting place. She meets the reader here and offers a hand:

> *the way the earth simply consents*
> *to season, night and day and*
> *altogether in space*

—BRUCE HERMAN, *artist and former Lothlórien Distinguished Chair in the art department of Gordon College*

There are threads of redemption running through the poetry of this book carrying joy tinged with beauty. Leslie's brilliantly crafted verse reveals her love for all creation. It is enriched by the light and beauty she finds everywhere—from the grace of a sandy beach to the paintings of Cézanne. She is as mindful of the smallest details of a butterfly flirting with a flower as she is with the immense presence of the winter tree, dark and naked outside her window. And who could not love her appreciation for what is as common and ordinary as the soup she makes on a winter's day? But what makes Leslie's poetry more deeply relevant is another thread that carries the faint tinge of illness and death. She stares into the hard facts of cancer with its unpredictable evil accompanied by its unpronounceable drugs. Her faith is not sentimental, rather it is strong enough to stand against the dark possibilities of her future.

—MARGIE HAACK, *author of The Place Trilogy*

Leslie Bustard is a true poet, and these poems are the real thing. Their surfaces are bright and beautiful, but there are hidden depths, rich and ringing, beneath the bright. I will read and reread these poems for the rest of my life.
—CHRISTIE PURIFOY, *author of* Placemaker

Leslie Bustard's poetry is beautiful not only because she stops long enough to notice things, but because she takes what she sees and opens our eyes to the extraordinary, ordinary world all around us. These are gifts: both her ability to see and the words that end up on the page, poems that are alive and invite us all into a deeper experience of living.
—SHAWN SMUCKER, *author of* The Day the Angels Fell

Leslie Bustard's new poems are the stuff of a visionary reality, penetrating beyond life's surfaces in the most generous way, expectant, full of the juice of a life of active reflection. She sees a scar as a sign of hope—grace celebrated in the midst of anguish. These poems illustrate so well how a poet penetrates beyond such surfaces (though even those surfaces have significance), opening up thoughtful responses to ordinary events, and finding ways to celebrate these "ordinaries" that are far from ordinary. I especially loved the poems that are clues to the generous work of God growing Leslie's soul, shaping her life-long focus on the beautiful ordinary.

I enjoyed reading these aloud, listening my way into them, almost hearing Leslie's voice. I suggest you do the same, and give glory to God for the way her words join together to create something entirely new and healing in your own reader's life.

Hail Leslie, full of grace, write on and invite us deeper into your challenging, grace-filled life.
—LUCI SHAW, *poet and author of* Angels Everywhere,
    The O in Hope, *and* Reversing Entropy (*2024*)

Leslie Bustard is a wonder woman of words. Life is a mosaic of details and she names them—the kitchen table, the butterfly bush, the cancer medicines. Each poem helps me see, feel, ache, and hope. I love this book and I love her!
—ANDI ASHWORTH, *author of* Real Love for Real Life:
   The Art and Work of Caring

These are poems that are ardently porous to the wonders of the world, insistent on its plain poetic beauty, unafraid of its mystery. The art of the poems is their appearance of unworked candour (in itself a hard-wrought skill), a transparency of heart, and an unwavering belief in the transcendent that lingers in this imminent realm. Beautiful, hopeful, honest, true to the grain of grace—this is a book to open the heart and the eye, giving us back marvel and joy in the land of the living.
—ANDREW ROYCROFT, *pastor/poet and author of*
   33: Reflections on the Gospel of John

Leslie Bustard is a miracle. In the throes of a grueling battle with cancer, when many of us might be tempted to turn inward or sullen, she has turned outward, grown brighter and effervesced reams of poetry. Tangible news of her mortality opens her eyes, inspires close inspection of trees, flowers, birds, skies, and the people in her life that mean so much to her. Dealing with cancer has brought the moments of her life suddenly, shimmeringly to life. Though she devotes quite a bit of energy to looking at paintings and engaging other authors, Bustard's own words are the starry night we didn't expect. She joins Sarah who, she writes, *was barren no more and all / her sadness had come untrue.* Constant joy. May we all aspire to this condition, in rich communion with God and all the Saints, fully healed in the grace of Jesus.
—AARON BELZ, author of *Soft Launch* (Persea, 2019)

THE GOODNESS OF THE LORD IN THE LAND OF THE LIVING

THE GOODNESS OF THE LORD IN THE LAND OF THE LIVING

SELECTED POEMS BY
LESLIE ANNE BUSTARD

SQUARE HALO BOOKS

©2023 Square Halo Books, Inc.
P.O. Box 18954
Baltimore, MD 21206
www.SquareHaloBooks.com

Front cover: *Addison's Walk* by Michelle Berg Radford
Back cover: *La Montagne Sainte-Victoire* by Paul Cézanne

ISBN 978-1-941106-31-0
Library of Congress Control Number: 2022949739

Printed in the United States of America

To Ned, my dear and loving husband,
I echo the words of Anne Bradstreet
to her husband:

If ever two were one, surely we ...
Thy love is such I can no way repay;
The heavens reward thee manifold, I pray.
Then while we live, in love let's so persever,
That when we live no more, we may live ever.

contents

foreword

In "The Ring of Time," E.B. White describes the work of a writer
as that of a secretary or custodian. "I have always felt charged," he
confesses, "with the safekeeping of all unexpected items of worldly
or unworldly enchantment, as though I might be held personally
responsible if even a small one were to be lost." White's concern
that we could lose enchanted realities is a perennial one, but it is
particularly pressing in our age of distraction when so many things
vie for our attention. How easily are we diverted. How easily do
the fast, bright, and pragmatic seduce us away from the good, true,
and beautiful. How easily is the spell broken. Thankfully, we have
writers like White among us today. We have those who understand
their work as curating, not simply words, but attention. We have
those called to safeguard what the rest of us miss. We have seers.

The word *seer* conjures up realms of myth and metaphysics;
indeed, to be a seer is to be a conjurer, to live in a world of mystery
and magic, to have seemingly supernatural sight. But perhaps, being
a seer is simpler than all that. Perhaps a seer is just someone who sees,
who notices what the rest of us overlook. If so, then the line between
writing and magic is much thinner than any of us understand.
For what is the work of writing except the work of seeing?

Leslie Bustard is one such seer, a woman gifted with what my
mountain neighbors call "the Sight." Like others before her, Leslie
has the ability to see beyond the world's appearances to its realities
and in doing so, remind us of its enchantment. With this, her first
collection of poems, Leslie does the work of safekeeping, pointing
our eyes back to those "unexpected items of worldly or unworldly
enchantment" that we dare not lose. May you find, as I have, that the
gift of her words is bested only by the gift of her sight.

—HANNAH ANDERSON, *author of* Turning of Days:
 Lessons from Nature, Season, and Spirit

SPRING

unHISTOrIC acTS

the growing good of the world is partly dependent
on unhistoric acts . . .
  George Eliot

Like many prayers that are said for the sick,
and thoughtful meals given after a baby is born.
Or when friends come to paint old walls
and fix broken steps.

As in listening ears and encouraging words.
Cards and flowers sent on hard days.
Trucks for moving furniture.

The grandmother who watches her daughter's
children, sharing her days with them.
And all those who mow their neighbors' lawns
and drive them to the pharmacy . . .

The goodness of the Lord in the land of the living.

Easter '57

Easter '57
is scribbled on the back
of a torn black and white—
her Sunday dress blown by
a breeze, his face caught
between a squint and a stare.

My mom was ten then.
In a few years the farm
they labored hard for would
fail, the cows would be sold
and a house in town bought.
Her mother would fall sick
and her dad grow weary.

Thirty years later, we
headed down south to find
their gravestone, like their farm,
well-tended and tidy.
The house in town was lost
to wild weeds and decay.

Mom once told me she saw
her dad in my brother—
both dark-haired and lanky.

And me—I don't have much
else but a few stories
and my love for a black
and white of two people
standing straight and tall on
a sunny, windy day
of Easter '57.

4

QUIET I

A robin's egg in a nest,

a row of yellow tulips, petals closed,

the last few shadowed moments
on the eastern horizon,

and Holy Saturday,
as Christ was lying in the sealed tomb,
    and angels were waiting.

QUIET II

That moment before sleep takes over,
I slowly free fall
into a yawning, empty space,

and for a few minutes,
all I hear is whir of wind
as it rattles old window panes,
the ring of a neighbor's chimes,
and rain on the porch roof.

I'll keep falling like Alice
who tumbled into Wonderland
then land shoeless on the street
in front of my childhood home.

Here God and his angels sit
behind clouds,
the moon hangs low and brightly amber.
I'll find a hiding place
near flowering honeysuckle,
where only the Holy Ghost can find me.

Burning Bush

Spring's blooming forsythia,
with its yellow branches reaching
up and out,
is a burning bush
    commanding attention.

But what if this bush had been cut back
with pruning shears—shaped into a neat
square, its brightness restrained?

As if the one who revealed his glory
on the mountain could be tamed,
and his words trimmed down to be less
    wild and demanding.

silver spring lake

There are no two roads
that diverge in this wood,
just one uneven dirt path
heading through trees—
with the lake on the right,
   and blue skies in branches above.

You tuck my hand in yours.
We speak slow words
   of an uncertain future.

Up ahead,
I see a fairy house at a tree's roots
   and place an acorn cap by its door.
Further on, our path slopes
   slippery from Thursday's rain.

Your arm reaches around my waist;
my hand holds your shoulder.
We find our way to level ground.
At a clearing in the trees,
we come into an open expanse—
   lake in view, and
   clouds reflected in its stillness.

May I stand here long,
leaning against you,
until we have to move on,
until we have to reach
   the end of the road.

THAT SENSE OF HOPE
(FOR SHAWN AND MAILE)

How your bare feet feel on soft grass,
hard ground underneath;

Those sweet juices of an orange
filling your mouth;

That tenor note halfway through *Lux Æterna*
which always makes your heart yearn;

But also heavy morning mist
before the sun opens up the curve in the road.

Hope is now the long wait,
holding onto the one unseen who yet sees.

JOHN 15:5

Quiet rustling of leaves,
wisps of wing and song,
        and above us,
    birds find shelter in
the tangle of overflowing wisteria.

And just maybe
        it is
    branches fruitful on the vine
providing those little birds of the air
the abundance they were promised.

summer

invitation

As if pursuing blue skies,
then diving, skimming with swift
shadows rippling across
the lake's surface
was a call to *come*

and follow,
two black swallows arch
within my view—once, twice, and
back again.

CLOUDS
(FOR WANT OF A BETTER TITLE)

I try to put words together about clouds,
   only *rolling billows* and
   streaks of pink
feel dull, overused.

The other day, clouds in our front window
looked like Michelangelo's voluptuous bodies.
Surprised, I called you over to see them with me.

At St. Peter's Basilica three summers ago,
we stood together under the ceiling's panoply of
   shapes and colors and movement.
I leaned against you to support my head tilted
upwards as I corralled all those fleshy, floating
images into my memory.

While we were leaving the chapel,
   we stared at the high altar wall.
Frescoed blue circled around a cast
of bodies upon bodies watching Jesus intently
as he and Mary descended on a cloud.

I saw that blue this morning.
The sky was empty—
save for one small cloud, stretched out
like sheared sheep's wool that had been
carded and cleaned,
waiting to be spun.

MY scar

The scar on my right breast and empty space under the skin
are reminders of last summer's surgery.

A nurse shared that after the surgeon removed the growing tumor,
his tiny stitches would fade to a faint trace of a curve.

Yet I was willing to bear any scar if it could be a down payment
on saving my breast or extending my life.

Like a delicate chain or
a thin, nearly invisible rainbow arching over my pink areola,
this scar is barely perceptible.

I want it to be a sign of hope, a symbol of promise:
    all may be well.

THE WAY THINGS ARE

I

Cancer hides in darkness—billeted inside.
If not dealt with, tumors will wreak havoc
in unknown places around my body.

II

The other day, as I turned onto Barley Mill Road,
I caught a glimpse of a single tiny ash leaf.
A yellow glow skimming the breeze.

III

Each afternoon this week,
a monarch returns to my butterfly bush.
Its orange wings flirting with the flowers.

IV

Rays of light dispersing through green-filled
branches, flowering morning glories, and
quick flights of swallows in the early night sky,

and Jesus.

MYSTERIES OF THE WORLD PART ONE

I

On hot summer nights,
after chasing a sprinkle of fireflies,
I would stretch out on my bed—
sheets pushed to the edge—
and wait for a breeze to make
its way through my screens.
It seemed all the mysteries of the world
floated on the trill of katydids.

I I

On bright summer days,
I would squint at a pile of clouds,
squeeze honeysuckle juice into my mouth,
watch a red ladybug travel the palm of my hand—
these were secrets of the universe.
The rattling wheels of roller-skating,
sounds of a neighbor boy playing his piano,
an empty carcass of a cicada hanging on our porch door—
these wonders hung in the air, as
I cartwheeled through the yard before dinner.

MYSTERIES OF THE WORLD PART TWO

I remember little-girl-me
walking up and down
my neighborhood street,
searching the summer sky.
I believed God and Jesus,
Adam and Eve and winged angels
sat behind all those piles of clouds.
Glory peeked through crevices,
as they watched the world go by.

Heading west on Delta,
flying above earth,
resting my forehead
against a window,
I scan peaks and canyons
and oceans of sunlit white,
waiting to see what is there.

MYSTERIES OF THE WORLD PART THREE

On this blue-sky summer day,
as clouds spill over,
I peek through the wooden slats
of my garden door
and take a long, slow look
at this little patch of world.

Two house finches feast
at their feeder; several house sparrows
(or maybe Carolina wrens)
line up on a wire overhead, watching.

A huge hosta plant
with tall lavender flowers
hosts a hunting bumblebee.

Pumpkin plants
have overrun the back garden bed,
and butterfly bush branches are a tangle
of white.

Flowering mint, purple coneflowers,
and near-blooming black-eyed Susans
lean toward the sun to
play their seasonal parts.

Two ghost-like cabbage moths flirt
and race around

just like they did last summer.

ode to summer in my backyard

How much land does a man need?
  Leo Tolstoy

Enough space for a monarch to flutter
around the butterfly bush in the backyard
and then flit away, only to return—
as if it had forgotten more sweet nectar could be found.
And enough lawn for white clover
to scatter around the grass, and for a few
bumble bees to shimmy and hum
over pink-tinged florets.

A little bit more land for shadows of
trees and their branches to come and go,
sway and disappear throughout the day.
There needs to be space for a raspberry bush and
a patch of black-eyed Susans
(that will fall over by mid-August); also,
some soil to grow basil for fresh pasta sauce and
rosemary for roasted potatoes.
To make iced tea and lemonade—
an ever expanding tangle of mint.

And for the wooden table and chairs
my daughters gifted me last spring,
a stone patio. Here we will share early evenings
of harvest-fresh meals and happy laughter.
I'll place flowerpots with bright
red geraniums and pink peonies close by.
Ants will scurry about, as
fireflies float up and away to the stars.

Delicious

When the glow of morning
runs through our faded, yellow curtains.

Or when car windows are rolled down,
and we are swallowed up
by the sun on open back roads
of farm country.

When I'm lying in green grass,
face to the shining blue sky,
both eyes squinting through upheld fingers,
and bright rays warming my skin.

BEACH DAY

A large storm off the southern coast is
churning water, and pushing it up the beach,
straight for our towels and chairs.
After a few times pulling up and moving back,
we finally skirt the day's surprising high tide.

And isn't this our life?
We have staked our place,
only to see, out on the horizon,
the path of trouble leads to us.

LIGHT I

The path of the righteous is like the light of dawn
that shines brighter and brighter until full day ...
        Proverbs 4:18

As when it finds its way down around
a maze of hydrangea leaves—
    almost unseen and
landing soft on my garden bed floor;

Or when the last of the morning dew
glistens quietly in a patch of our yard
as the sun reveals itself through
topmost branches of our neighbor's tree,
brightening green maple leaves
above my head ...

a reminder that sometimes a light surprises.

LIGHT II

Sometimes a light surprises . . .
William Cowper

like tonight when I
stepped into the crisp night air,
then, looking up, was
startled by a trail of light
passing through the blue-black sky.

THE WORD OF THE LORD CAME TO US

You say we are
   stars
   sand
   salt.

You call us
   living stones
   living sacrifices

We are made ready by you
Living Water.

You name us
Oaks of Righteousness
   grounding
   rooting
   building us
into the House of the LORD,

so we can declare you
Good.

BUDDLEJA

Every yellow round droplet
down the center of each
white flower on
each flowering
branch

of my butterfly bush
makes me imagine
the Creator
deciding

to use the tiniest dropper
to place spots of yellow
that fill all the
hidden

stamens on all the flowered
bushes in the world;
and I am in awe
once

again.

autumn

RaTHFriLanD MorninG

And some time make the time to drive out west ...
In September or October, when the wind
And the light are working off each other ...
      Seamus Heaney

Or one morning make time to brave moody skies.
Call the Collie to your side as you walk
to the pond—you will find the farmers' lane
is quiet with Holly Blue butterflies
above the hedgerow and occasional
warblings of a wren. Honeysuckle
will be blooming bright among hawthorn and
ripe blackberries. Land, like clouds,
will spread far beyond. Stand still at a pasture gate
and wait for cows to meander near.
Their soft eyes will look up from eating, and
one by one they'll gather to you, jostling
to be closer. At the end of the lane,
two swans glide away from tall grass,
small cygnets following slowly behind,
as if distracted by all that shines.

CARLINGFORD LOUGH Prayer, 09.21

That part of Rostrevor which overlooks Carlingford Lough
is my idea of Narnia.
    C.S. Lewis in a letter to Warnie, his brother

The tide was low that early evening we
meandered along the beach of Carlingford Lough.

Cockle shells and limpet shells sat among
a scattered still life of seaweed and slate pebbles.

I picked up a bleached shell, its high arch so smooth
my thumb moved easily to worrying the inside.

Placing it rib-side down in my palm,
it looked ready to catch the last of the sun's rays—

just like my hands in prayer,
upturned.

CRASH COURSE

I take a piece of white paper
from the pile on the kitchen table,
and a lone red magic marker,
and fill its space with tall capital letters—
    I love you.

After a few attempts at creasing
and folding, I google *how*
to make a paper airplane—
though you showed our children this
maybe an hour ago.

I want to see my airplane glide
into your hand after one sweeping loop
in the air but imagine it will nose-dive
into an elbow and crash land at your feet.

Outside, taking a cue from one of our girls,
I hold the paper airplane above my head,
and pointing it, walk over to you
in the middle of our yard.

THE BIRD OUT MY WINDOW

as hawks rest upon air, and
the air sustains them . . .
    Denise Levertov

I keep returning in my mind
to a bird I saw yesterday.
She sat still on the topmost branch
of a nearby tree made leaf–empty
by a late autumn rain.
Of all places to perch,
this bird chose the thinnest,
loneliest twig.
With no other birds nearby,
she tightly held her own
against a white sky.
Her weight,
or a slight breeze,
caused the branch to sway.
With a tilt of her small head
and ruffle of feathers,
she looked side to side,
content,
so far away from solid ground.
I keep wondering:
is this what it's like to
be a sparrow in God's eyes . . .
peacefully perched up high,
confident that letting go
will not result in free fall?
I recall looking away for a moment
. . . then she was gone.

samaras I

Like whirligigs flying fast from children's hands,
our maple tree's seedpods fill the early autumn air.

They land without fanfare,
making a mosaic of the backyard.

During summer days, they stuck to my bare feet
and my puppy's tail
and found their way into the house,
under the kitchen table, in between floorboards,
up to the bedrooms—

reminding me of seeds the Good Sower scattered
generously over his land.

Today,
I was startled by a sapling in my neighbor's garden,
a shoot not weeded this spring,
    standing straight
    growing towards the sun
    bearing the beauty of new leaves.

samaras II

Whirling maple seedpods,
spinning a race to the ground,
are a picture of living in the moment.
They land green and flat,
as if they know their life
will be spent growing or dying.

samaras III

Clusters of Japanese maple seedpods
hang loosely on my neighbor's tree.
Each pod's skin tinged pink—
hinting at new life.

THE Tree across THE STReeT

Let us stretch ourselves out towards him,
that when he comes he may fill us full.
    Augustine

The tree across the street,
the one I see framed in our front window,
was slowly losing its leaves,
until yesterday's wind came.
Now only a scattering of red and orange remain,
exposing a maze of branches

reaching out,
stretching up.

And then there is my heart,
how gradually I reveal it
to me   to you

to God.

How my longings reach out
and then stretch
and stretch up,
waiting to be filled.

And in spring,
the tree I see in our window shines
by afternoon sun,
rich with its pink flowers
and its green leaves.

33

tonsure

Like me, with my skin
and scar exposed, did newly-
vowed monks think of rain
and wind on their bare heads as
reminders of Christ with them?

cancer: almost year three

If we hope for what we do not see,
We wait for it with patience. Romans 8:25

Early morning autumn light—
loosened yellow maple leaves
float like flecks of gold on air;
My shadow lengthens long.

And the sun warms the crown
of my hair-empty head.

This, the feeling of hope.

winter

TO make VISIBLe

To make visible,
glory;
for a moment
see the mystery of eternity
in our ordinary.
To long for the light
and to let it sweep
through shadowed windows,
waiting hearts.
To listen.
To say yes,
let it be as you say it will be.
To wait till the word breaks in,
revealing grace
upon grace upon grace.

BE STILL

The LORD will fight for you; you need only to be still.
    Exodus 14:14 NIV

My drug of choice is Benadryl—
pure, in its liquid form, and
shot straight into my port.
I can count backward from ten,
and then find myself
disconnected from my head,
heavy and sleepy.
I need a multitude of drugs
to attack this cancer,
ones I can hardly spell or pronounce.
There is Anastrozole and Encorafenib
and Binimetinib.
But Benadryl puts me to sleep
while Kanjinti courses through me—
so that I can say to God,
    I was still while you fought for me.

12 noon, mid-february

Quiet morning snow gave way
to the patter of ice rain
on our roof and window sills.

When it stopped,
a faraway chatter of birds
filled the silence.

I could picture them in a tree
all bunched together,
feathers fluffed up.

Their beaks opening and closing,
their words incessant—
possibly a cheer for a reprieve from rain.

A thought of April floated through my mind—
of green and birds and flowers,
of spring showers and umbrellas.

Rain started again,
but the birds kept chattering.
And above them,

the caw   caw   caw of a lone blackbird,
and the peals of an old church bell
chiming noon.

A Poem for Lent

With February full of family birthdays
and Valentine's Day,
Lent usually finds me unprepared.
I've spent my energy on presents and chocolate.

I realize the season of repentance has begun
when I see smudged crosses on my neighbors' foreheads
and hear what friends are giving up for forty days.

But me, my hands are empty,
and I'm already repenting of forgetfulness.

It's a little like heading to my tool shed on a Saturday morning,
ready to prepare for spring planting,
only to realize I've forgotten to replace the rusty, cracked shovel
and broken green hose.

What a grace to arrive Easter day singing
Alleluia.
And what a glory to see the yellow of forsythia
and tulips blooming red.

THUISDaY

Sunday night when I learned there was more cancer,
that a year of fighting had not held off another tumor,

the place inside me where I imagine my emotions reside
was a yawning cavern, empty.

I decided it was denial, and let myself sleep long
and nap and wander around.
I thought of other people praying.

But today,
with the expanse of blue sky above me
and the silver drip of icicles I passed while walking the dog,

I know I must be waking up.

For, as I walked into the kitchen,
I thought of soups I want to make and
cookies I want to bake.

I looked for the Dickens book packed away in the basement.
I thought of pencil and paper and images and words.

I even hung the wooden red-and-white heart sign
from last Valentine's Day and
made dinner for you and me.

Trees along my way

Trees in winter,
naked and exposed,

look as if they are a tangle of hands reaching up—
limbs and branches taking hold of the sun for warmth
and grabbing at blue sky for cover.

And as the sun goes down,
when sky holds indigo before it falls to black,
they are a silent silhouette of waiting.

THE END OF WINTER

Leaf-empty oak trees—
their profiles resting
on blue-dusky skies—
invite a lingering look
over their lines, their stillness.
They ask us to consider our
souls, exposed to this wide world,
and to make space for coming
birds and their nests,
to listen for the wind's hum,
and to capture light
as it makes its way
down to our taproots.

HINTS OF a LONGED-FOR, FAR-OFF COUNTRY

I pulled out the tree
we spotted in a row of freshly cut Frasers
at Frey's and breathed in—
as if for the first time—
its sweet pine scent.

We set it up by
our front window, with its hundreds
of twinkling lights
reflecting back in the darkened glass.

BLESSING

Every Sunday,
after receiving
bread and wine,
we hear,
"Listen to the Lord's
benediction."

We lift up our
hands; we open
our eyes. In front
of me with her
little arms out
wide and her palms
upturned, fingers
strumming the air,
is Jubilee.

The pastor's words
wind their way through
us like a fall
breeze stirring
tall trees outside.

It moves in and
out, leaf-empty
branches stretching
up to take in
each ray of light,
while deep down roots
intertwine.

EKPHrasis
Poems

AFTER REMBRANDT'S
SIMEON AND ANNA IN THE TEMPLE

. . . and a sword shall pierce through your soul.
   Luke 2:35

Maybe Mary missed those shocking details
Simeon spoke as she looked at Jesus in
his ancient arms. With her memories of
angels and shepherds, one could understand
any weariness at unexpected
words. Except, she was in the habit of
listening to astonishing and strange
prophecies—as if she knew the ways of
the world were revealed through donkeys and old
men. (I think I would have asked one or two
questions and maybe for a timeline.) Yet
young Mary had been learning that even
as a small candle breaks the shadowed dark,
hard paths are lightened by sustaining grace.

After Rouault's
CHRIST AND THE WOMAN SAINT

I could be that woman kneeling before Christ.
As he leans in, his eyes look for mine.
I bend my head, unsure of his gaze.
His hand offers me a quiet invitation.
Yes, this could be me. It could be Rachel weeping
or Mary sitting at Christ's feet.
Or it could be my daughter, my mother, or
my neighbor. Here is Jesus saying, "Come
to me for rest, all you who are weary."
Woman, for you, too, he offers his hand.

AFTer ROUAULT'S
CHRIST AND THE CHILDREN

These little ones dance
around Jesus—the ones he
just blessed; laughing and
singing, they are unaware
that it is their faith we need.

After Rouault's
APPEARANCE ON THE ROAD TO EMMAUS

[Rouault's] angle is 'angelic'—half way between heaven and earth.
  Makoto Fujimura

Things into which angels long to look:

Cleopas, learning that Jesus was no longer in the tomb,
walked with a friend to Emmaus from Jerusalem

and then listened to a stranger speak
surprising words concerning Christ.

That day was bright and sharp—
bursting into spring-life with its blues, and greens, and reds.

Each single blade of grass, each flower,
each step on the path
proclaimed a new promise to those burning hearts.

At a table spread with bread and wine,
his eyes would be opened,
and a stranger would be revealed.

AFTer paul cézanne's
MONT SAINTE-VICTOIRE

. . . beautiful in elevation, is the joy of all the earth, Mount Zion,
in the far north, the city of the great King.
    Psalm 48:2

To have not been left waiting and lonely
At the foot of the mountain would have been
Enough, but he led us to his holy
House, welcoming us in, his very kin.
Tears once flooded our faces; shaming night
Shadows filled our thoughts. Now his very hands
Wash us clean; each memory bathed by light.
He gathers multitudes of those from lands
Of every time and tongue. Yet more he shares
When he beckons us to enjoy fine wine
And meat of his table—he nothing spares.
With his invitation to *ask* and *find,*
We drink living water, gladdened by springs
Which offer us peace to rest and to sing.

AFTer PauL CÉzanne's
APPLES AND ORANGES

As if these colors could heal me of indecision once and for all . . .
  Rainer Maria Rilke, 1907

Cézanne arranged his still life with much thought,
having planned each detail of the table
with its white cloth, jug, and bowl. The apples
and oranges placed in their own spots. He
took pleasure in seeing the reds with the
greens and the blues with the yellows, and how
these colors conversed quietly among
themselves. Painting was a simple act of
love, one that held on, continued. His work
came from here. Oh Lord, how to live like that.

AFTer PauL CÉzanne's
VUE SUR L'ESTAQUE ET LE CHÂTEAU D'IF

I wanted to tell you about all this, because it connects in a
hundred places ... and with ourselves ...
   Rainer Rilke on Paul Cézanne, 1907

Staring straight through the parted trees, into
the colors of l'Estaque, I want to grab
your hand, step through the frame. We'll walk
down the path, race over the red roofs, then
freestyle down into those blues and greens.

Around the Marseille Bay we float,
content and satisfied, and only slightly sunburnt.

after Monet's
THE MAGPIE

Snow is falling from the night
sky, like dust escaping from
a nebula above, leaving
all Étretat covered
paper-white, from
the farmer's land to
a wide pale-pearled horizon.

An old long roof and
the boundary wall's slate
stones bear the layered weight.

Early morning light
will tickle the trees' skeletal branches,
and noon will see blue-grey shadows
stretch across the ground.

A small, solitary magpie perches on the gate,
alert to what the day has offered—
as if there is no need
to fill the air with chatter.

AFTER ANDREW WYETH'S
PENNSYLVANIA LANDSCAPE

It always seems to happen.

I find myself left behind,
too slow for those I've come with.

Pennsylvania Landscape hangs right before me
at the room's entrance—
   familiar curve of land
   quiet farmhouse
   a large, looming sycamore
reach out, pull me in.

I slowly trace all the white and brown
bare limbs with my eyes.
Each branch is its own self
and each limb attached to others.

I scan the gray-white sky
brooding close behind crisscrossed boughs

and hope the house down the hill
has an unlocked door and
a light left on.

AFTER ANDREW WYETH'S
AIRBORNE

The wind ... you cannot tell where it comes from or where it is going.
So it is with everyone born of the Spirit.
   Jesus to Nicodemus

Those feathers came on the air,
tumbling and sliding: wind
underneath and around them—
filling space above the long yard,
moving on to someplace and somewhere.
The breeze without a path;
the anemometer broken.
White and gray curiosities flying forward
from nowhere we could see,
then landing on the rock wall,
dipping in the pond,
and hiding in the tall rushes.

A poet once asked, "Who has seen the wind?"
Jesus reminded a Jewish scholar,
"The wind blows wherever it pleases."
And what if these windows were opened,
and those feathers blew through, settling
on the old wood floor and crumbling mantle?
If our glance slanted sideways for a moment,
we might witness the mystery of angels passing by
or the Holy Spirit's work
of awakening all that is dead to new life.

aFTer Andrew WYeTH'S
PENTECOST

We've worked all night and caught nothing, but I will do as you say.
   Peter

Was Peter's mind racing when the net
was so full it almost ripped,
or when he hung it between the poles,
with the breeze off the sea
moving through its brown lines?
Did he run his hands over the frayed cords
as Jesus said, "Follow me and fish for men"?
What did he think when he saw twelve baskets of fish?
Or when night waves overwhelmed the boat,
and he stepped out, surrounded by high winds?

Days after the curtain tore in two,
what filled his thoughts in the still of the morning,
as he heard, "Throw your net to the right!"
What did he think when the net—
with a hundred-fold fish—did not rip?
And later, when the sound of wind roared
through the upper room,
what did Peter remember as he preached,
"It will be in the last days, says God,
I will pour out my Spirit on all people"?

Was it the net, fish-full, that did not rip?

56

aFTer AnDrew WYeTH's
WIND FROM THE SEA

Sometimes you've got to open up the window
and let the wind blow through ...
    Douglas Kaine McKelvey

The window had been left open during the night.
One could see beyond the wide expanse of yard
to dark tree lines and sliver of silver sea.
A lacey curtain hanging over ripped shade
was light enough to catch even a slight breeze off the water.
But today—this white-clouded day—
the wind came sudden and strong; and the curtain,
with its torn edges flew into the room—
like a ghost: hovering, waiting.

Spirit, come.
Awake in us
all that is worn and weary.

FOUND
POEMS

After exploring Cézanne's paintings, German poet
Rainer Maria Rilke shared his discoveries with his wife:

After Rilke, Oct. 7, 1907

Here,
all of reality is on his side—
in his dense quilted blue
and the reddish black of his wine bottles,

[Here]
the humbleness of his observations—
the apples are cooking apples,
and the wine bottles belong in
the bulging pockets of an old coat . . .

After Rilke, Oct. 13, 1907

. . . these colors could heal me of all indecision.

The good conscience of these reds, these blues—
their simple truthfulness educates you.
And if you stand among them,
you get the impression they are doing something for you.

AFTER RILKE, OCT. 19,1907

One can find examples among his earlier works
where he surpasses himself to achieve
the utmost capacity for love—

   a simple life of love which endures.

How very much of one piece is everything
we encounter; how related one thing is to the next.
All we basically have to do is be there,
simply, ardently—

   the way the earth simply consents
   to season, night and day and
   altogether in space.

AFTer EDITH STein,
THe SOUL OF a woman
(WITH RESPONSE)

The soul of a woman
must be expansive,
open to all human beings,
quiet so no weak flame will be extinguished,
warm so not to benumb fragile buds,

[and] empty of itself
in order that extraneous life
may have room in it;

and finally
mistress of [herself]
and [her] body,
so that the entire person is
readily at the disposal of every call.

My soul would be shriveled to stillness;
my eyes staring into waters of Narcissus and
my life bound to nothingness—
but you, Jesus,
would not let it be so.
Light and life and freedom
you poured into me.
My soul is rooted and enlarged
because of you, Christ.
As you are for me,
may I be for those you give me.

After E.B. White,
An Approach to Style

Place yourself in the background.
     E.B. White

Young writers often suppose that style
is a garnish for the meat of prose,
a sauce by which a dull dish is made palatable.
Style has no separate entity;
it is nondetachable, unfilterable.
The beginner should approach style warily,
realizing it is an expression of self.

Writing becomes a question of learning
to make occasional wing shots,
bringing down the bird of thought
as it flashes by.

The writer is a gunner
in the blind, waiting
for something to come in—
sometimes [having cultivated patience]
roaming the countryside
hoping to scare something up . . .

to bring down
one partridge.

After E.B. White, Gravity

it seems as though no laws—
not even fairly old ones—
can safely be regarded as unassailable

the force of gravity—
which we have always ascribed to
the "pull of the earth"—
was reinterpreted
by a scientist who says
when we fall
it is not earth pulling us,
it is heaven pushing us

this blasts the rock on which we sit

if science can do a right about-face
on a thing so fundamental as gravity
maybe Newton was a sucker
not to have just eaten the apple

tanka
poems

(31 syllables; 5 lines;
5
7
5
7
7

AT Tea WITH a Friend

"I haven't written
in weeks," I said. "I think all
I can write about
are birds or trees." *"Sounds like the
start of a poem,"* she said.

ISAIAH 35:1

A fir tree's fresh scent—
a hint that one day streams of
living water will
flow through the wilderness and
the deserts will blossom bright.

ISAIAH 41:19

We should have a land of trees.
Langston Hughes

When the banquet is
set high on God's mountain, I
hope our view is the
trees—the cedars and cypress
planted by springs of water.

Matthew 1:19–25

Today I often
imagine Joseph's courage
to give up his life
for Mary and also how
you follow in Joseph's ways.

Song of Songs 2:10

My beloved spoke and said to me,
 "Arise, my darling,
  my beautiful one, come with me."

I have learned to hear
God call me his Beloved
because your love for
me is the parable he
wrote to teach me to believe.

Luke 19:40

When words stumble slow
from my pen, when dark covers
day too soon, and leaves
have left behind their trees, still,
stones will cry aloud your praise.

annunciation

... and the stillness the dancing.
　　T.S. Elliot

As if Mary's yes
opened the dark skies for the
light to appear and
to blink along smooth waters,
while kingfishers and herons
sat still, waiting for the dawn.

psalm 126:1–3

*God has made laughter for me; everyone
who hears will laugh with me.*
　　Sarah

"And the Lord kept his
promise," we'll say, our laughter
like Sarah's when she
was barren no more and all
her sadness had come untrue.

acorn
(FOR LUCI)

With smooth faces and
knubby caps, a few acorns
roll around in my palm, their
brown bodies a distraction—
in my pocket, a surprise.

blue

Cerulean sky
mirrored on today's calm seas
draws my eyes towards
the horizon, leading my
gaze upward into more blue.

carried
(FOR CAREY)

A kitten carried
in its mother's mouth, a cub
in the soft grip of
a lioness, and you, whose
hand I once held, in my heart.

DaFFODILS

Bright yellow heads on
long green stems stand tall in my
yard; I gather them
together, and tie them with
blue ribbon, ready for you.

EGGS

I bring a carton
of twelve brown speckled eggs home;
I love their round yolks
in my pan, but not when they
splatter on the kitchen floor.

FIre

Summertime means friends
around the fire pit as
it crackles with sparks
dancing up into the night
sky, and the moon clear and bright.

GOLDEN
(FOR MAGGIE)

"Golden" plays loud on
the radio as we drive
back roads; we sing out,
and I'm glad for your quick laugh
and the sparkle in your eyes.

HOLES

The hole in the sink,
the one I made and covered
with tape months ago,
makes me hope God is quicker
at fixing my brokenness.

IONA
(FOR ELSPETH IONA)

One rainy day, we
walked with you around ancient
places and old paths;
we made a memory of
your smiles and this green island.

jesus

Good Shepherd and Light
in the Darkness—I can walk
these shadowed paths and
valleys with courage because
you promise to be with me.

kite

A kite waltzes high
above the trees, its long line
tethered in my hand—
reminders to dance in the
wide space of God's gracious grip.

long

One cannot measure
an anxious heart—hope becomes
a long wait, stretching
into the watchful stillness
of the always now of God.

memory
(FOR NED)

One sunny morning
in June, I wore my long white
dress; it was a day
for songs and vows—and, yes, I
would say Yes to you again.

NO

Are we too quick to
say *no* to each other (like
toddlers who have
learned new words), forgetting the
yes and *amen* of Jesus?

overflow

Like a glass sitting
under a running faucet
spilling out with clear
water, so my cup flows
over with the wine of Christ.

penny

A penny for your
thoughts—a bright shiny copper
one—or maybe ten;
share your many cares with me . . .
I will be here to listen.

quiet

"Do not go gentle"
says the poet, but God says
 "I will quiet you
with love"—Spirit, after I've
raged, settle deep your comfort.

rain

The unceasing sound
of midnight rain on the roof
wakens me; I close
my eyes—its pitter patter
ebbs and flows into my dreams.

SUNLIGHT
(FOR ANNE BRADSTREET)

Bright morning sun has
flooded through these old windows,
fading our pine floors;
oh, how good the light that will
always dispel the darkness.

TULIPS
(AFTER THE PAINTING BULB FIELDS)

Color and light fill
Van Gogh's tulip fields—blocks of
pink, blue, and yellow
in quilt-like rows; each flower's
head a cup drinking sunshine.

UNDERNEATH

Happy is the one
who is like the child who climbed
high in a tree, but
knew underneath her faithful
father's strong arms still waited.

vines

In spring, green buds and
tiny leaves parade along the
vines on my fence; they
make me hopeful for the
fullness and fruit of summer.

waTer

Those dark waves roared, yet
you parted and stilled and walked
on them; now, Living
Water, reach out—free me from
the pull of the undertow.

X

X marks the spot on
a treasure map; and what more
could my heart long for
except to be a pearl of
God's, found and rejoiced over?

YELLOW
(FOR KAREN PERIS)

"Bright as yellow"—like
how the sun shines through leaf-filled
branches; its warm rays
are outstretched arms greeting you
and me with great shouts of joy.

ZED

Apples, acorns, zinc,
and zoo; A to Z (or zed)—
Alpha, Omega ...
from beginning to end, in
Christ all is held together.

BeneDICTION

We are filled with the good things of your house.
     Psalm 65:4 NIV

Morning sunshine filling the kitchen windows,
and a yellow knitted throw on my lap,

books lining our shelves,
and laughter around the table,

words in my head that I scribble on lined paper,
songs we sing together Sunday mornings,
water on a baby's head . . .

and every week,
Bread and Wine placed in my hand:
"the Body and Blood, given for you—
     take and eat."

Leslie Anne Bustard lives in a century-old row house in Lancaster City, PA, with her husband, Ned. Here they love to offer food and friendship to folks and collect a plethora of artwork, music, and books. She spent much of her adult years home-schooling her three girls and teaching literature, poetry, art appreciation, and writing to other children in various home-schooling co-ops. Leslie also taught middle school literature and writing at a local classical school, as well as produced high school and children's theater. She currently writes for The Cultivating Project, The Black Barn Online, Story Warren, and Calla Press. Leslie loves museum-ing and watching movies with her family. Her first book was *Wild Things and Castles in the Sky: A to Choosing the Best Books for Children* (Square Halo Books, 2022). You can find more of Leslie's musings at PoeticUnderpinnings. com and listen to her podcast at SquareHaloBooks.com.

special thanks

This book would not have been possible without the generosity of all of those who supported the crowdsourcing campaign. I am grateful to each and every supporter and would like to especially thank:

EPIC
PATRONS
Marlin & Laurie
Detweiler

EKPHrasis
PATRONS
Anna Cheng

Samantha Cabrera

Lauren Brown

Sean Lucas

Douglas McKelvey

Lancia E. Smith

Lisa Smith

Lynette Stone

Tanka
PATRONS
Amy Knorr

Jeremy Begbie

Kim Fisher

Amelia Freidline

Margie Haack

Laura Hittle

David & Kathy Knoll

Lisa Landis Blowers

Lee Lovett & Lois Theisen

Bailey McGee

Jennifer Owens

Christie Purifoy

Théa Rosenburg

Susan Smetzer-Anderson

Jennifer Smithfield

afterword

In October 2020, while I was dealing with the reality of cancer and the hard side effects of my medicines, a desire to write poetry grew within me. I turned to God with this deep-well-of-a-wish. For decades I have loved reading and sharing poetry with family and friends but had not written any of my own poems since I was a teenager. I am grateful for how God answered my prayer. This book is a witness of his goodness to me.

During college I discovered the Puritan poet Anne Bradstreet; she became not only American's first published poet but also my first favorite poet. I was excited to find a writer of Christian faith to whom I could relate. Like me, but in a different time and place, Anne wrestled in her heart as she sought God above all else and desired to trust him wholly.

Almost a decade after Anne Bradstreet left her mark, the poems of Luci Shaw became a means of grace to me. Through Luci's writings I experienced how poetry mysteriously opens one's eyes and heart to the things of the Spirit as well as to the beauty of nature. She helps me stay attentive to light, trees, blue sky, and other lovely things.

Lastly, the words and songs of Karen Peris have been part of the "soundtrack" of my life; I have been listening to her sing with her band since I was eighteen years old. Her writing made quiet ordinary life glow and gave me (and continues to give me) a vision of its goodness in my home and with my people.

Seamus Heaney, Malcolm Guite, and Billy Collins are also favorite poets. But these three women—Anne Bradstreet, Luci Shaw, and Karen Peris—have been used by God to enlarge my imagination and my desire for beauty, truth, and goodness.

I am thankful to all the kind people who have given to turn the *idea* of a book of my poetry into a *real* book. My thanks first to

Hannah Anderson—for her good and true words I have been reading for several years and for saying yes to writing this introduction. Secondly, to the tremendous people who wrote such amazing endorsements for the book—I am humbled and overjoyed! Finally (and most importantly), thanks to the ninety-two patrons who backed this book— I have been overwhelmed by your generosity. I am deeply grateful for all of these conduits of God's grace to me.

Lastly, a treasure trove of friends added their experiences and insights to my writing. When I needed help, I knew I had writers and poets to turn to. Thank you Théa Rosenburg, Christine Perrin, Amy Maslkeit, and Jessica Whipple. And then these friends—Linnea Krall, Kimberly Ibarra, Amy Knorr, Shawn and Maile Smucker, Katy Hutson, Diana Bauer, Lisa Smith, Lynette Stone, and, nearly every day, Ned—offered me such an abundance of encouragement in my writing and creative endeavors these past years, I could hardly hold it all in my heart.

Friends, may this book be a testimony to the goodness of the Lord in the land of the living. And may it, in some small way, help you to have eyes to see Him and his steadfast love for you.

—Leslie Anne Bustard
BookEnd, Autumn 2022

acknowledgments

These poems were written between October 2020–22
(with *Easter '57* being the one exception). Thank you to all
the friends who listened and read and encouraged me in my
poetic wanderings. The ABC tanka poems were first presented
in the Square Halo Gallery in 2021, lettered and illustrated
by my friend, artist Hannah Weston. And thank you to those
who published early versions of these poems:

AGAPE REVIEW: *I Corinthians 15:42, Quiet II, Buddleja* (previously titled
Attention to Details), *Psalm 126:1–3, Be Still* (previously titled *Being Quiet*)

AMETHYST REVIEW: *Long, Water, X*

CALLA PRESS: *Burning Bush, Ode to Summer, Invitation, Quiet I, After
Rouault's Christ and the Woman Saint, Unhistoric Acts* (appeared as
Ordinary Goodness)

SEEN JOURNAL: *A Poem for Lent, To Make Visible*

CLAYJAR REVIEW: *Jesus, Quiet*

CULTIVATING: *After Andrew Wyeth's Pennsylvania Landscape;
After Rouault's Christ and the Woman Saint; After Rouault's Christ and
the Children; After Rouault's Appearance on the Road to Emmaus; After
Claude Monet's Magpie; After Paul Cézanne's Mont-Sainte-Victoire; The End
of Winter* (first appeared as *Cultivating*); *The Tree Across the Street; Myster-
ies of the World II; After Rembrandt's Simeon and Anna in
the Temple; Easter '57; After E.B. White, An Approach to Style; After E.B.
White, Gravity; After Edith Stein, The Soul of a Woman; After Rilke, Oct. 17,
1907; After Rilke, Oct. 13, 1907; After Rilke, Oct. 19, 1907.*

FATHOM: *After Paul Cézanne's Apples and Oranges* (first appeared
as *What Rilke Taught Me*)

MORE GOODNESS FROM SQUARE HALO

WILD THINGS AND CASTLES IN THE SKY: A GUIDE TO CHOOSING THE BEST BOOKS FOR CHILDREN

Curated and edited by Leslie and Carey Bustard with Théa Rosenburg (a mother-daughter team and a children's books blogger), this book encourages and envisions parents, grandparents, teachers, and friends—to know the power of a good story and to share it with a child they love.

ORDINARY SAINTS: LIVING EVERYDAY LIFE TO THE GLORY OF GOD

Leslie Bustard and over forty other writers celebrate Square Halo's twenty-fifth anniversary with essays on such topics as homemaking, knitting, playlists, comic books, juggling, pipes, chronic pain, traffic, pretzels, and naps.

33: REFLECTIONS ON THE GOSPEL OF SAINT JOHN

Irish pastor-poet Andrew Roycroft's poems "let the light in, warming the heart with holiness and firing the imagination with life. Slow your step. Come and linger with the poet on the best of thoughts ... Christ."—Kristyn Getty

LIFTING THE VEIL: IMAGINATION AND THE KINGDOM OF GOD

Poet Malcolm Guite explores how the creative work of poets and other artists can begin to lift the veil, kindling our imaginations for Christ.

SQUAREHALOBOOKS.COM